A CRICKET BOOK®

Introduction

Get out your guitar or sit down at the piano, your child on your lap or your children gathered around you, and make music together! Here are all the songs that appeared in LADYBUG magazine in 1995: familiar Mother Goose songs, age-old folk songs, and other nursery favorites. We selected a few contemporary songs but mostly traditional ones, because you may remember some of them from your own childhood and be able to sing them without any instruments at all.

The special magic of our songs lies in the correspondence of musical notes on one page to the pictures on the other. One hundred years ago, two German brothers came up with the idea of writing down the most beloved children's songs not only in clear musical notation but also in little picture notes that corresponded exactly to the melody. When you sing or play the song, your child will be able to follow the melody by going up and down with the pictures. The longer or shorter notes are represented by larger or smaller figures. After a while it will be easy for your children to follow the picture melody and sing along with you and the entire family.

You'll find that it's great fun to sing together, to feel the rhythm and clap, rock, or dance to it. Children may want to invent their own words and rhythm games or actions or use their imaginations in making up new and often hilarious verses. The more fun and laughter, the better. Your children will come to look forward to "music time" and will ask to sing the songs again and again.

Marianne Carus, Editor-in-Chief

CONTENTS

Hop, Hop, Hop!

Traditional Children's Song

Art by True Kelley

Hop, hop, hop! Hop and nev - er stop.
Hop, my pret - ty lit - tle bun - ny.
You're so soft and sweet and fun ny.
Hop, hop, hop, hop, hop! Hop and nev - er stop.

Polar Bear and Crocodile
Words by David Stevens
Art by Nadine Bernard Westcott
American folk melody:
"Sweet Betsy from Pike"
We sing of the po-lar bear fear-less and bold. He
The croc - o - dile lives in the trop - i - cal belt. And
nev - er feels hot and he nev - er feels cold, Be-
nei - ther the cold nor the heat ev - er felt, Be-
cause where he lives sum-mer nev - er oc - curs, And the
cause in the win - ter his sum-mers be - gin, And the
rest of the year he wears plen-ty of furs.
rest of the year he wears croc-o-dile skin.

We sing of the po - lar bear fear - less and bold. He
The croc - o - dile lives in the trop - i - cal belt. And
nev - er feels hot and he nev - er feels cold, Be-
nei - ther the cold nor the heat ev - er felt, Because where he lives sum-mer nev - er oc - curs, And the
cause in the win - ter his sum-mers be - gin, And the
rest of the year he wears plen - ty of furs.
rest of the year he wears croc - o - dile skin.

Buddies and Pals

Traditional Children's Song • Art by Jennifer Plecas

The Caterpillar
Music by Emilie Poulsson
Words by Cornelia C. Roeske
C
Fuz - zy lit - tle cat - er - pil - lar, Crawl-ing, crawl-ing
G C A
on the ground, Fuz - zy lit - tle cat - er - pil - lar,
D7 G C F
No-where, no-where to be found, Tho' we've looked and
C G7 C
looked and hunt-ed, Ev-'ry-where a - round!

Art by Elizabeth E. Howard
Fuz - zy lit - tle cat - er - pil - lar, Crawl-ing, crawl-ing
on the ground, Fuz - zy lit - tle cat - er - pil - lar,
No-where, no-where to be found, Tho' we've looked and
looked and hunt - ed, Ev- 'ry- where a - round!
Turn the page
for more verses.

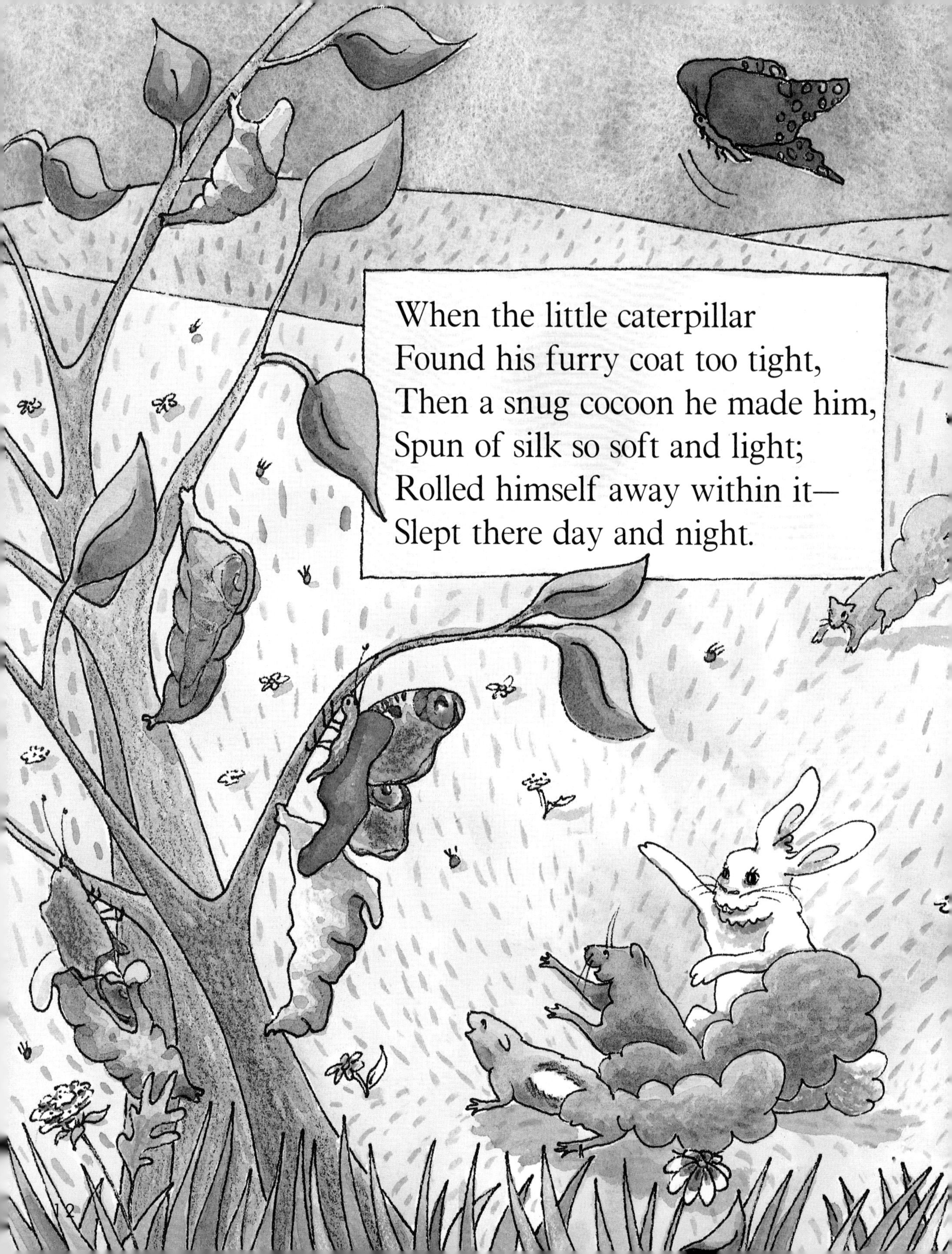

When the little caterpillar
Found his furry coat too tight,
Then a snug cocoon he made him,
Spun of silk so soft and light;
Rolled himself away within it—
Slept there day and night.

See how this cocoon is stirring—
Now a little head we spy.
What? Is this our caterpillar,
Spreading gorgeous wings to dry?
Soon the free and happy creature
Flutters gaily by.

I'm a Nut!
Traditional Nonsense Song
Art by Dominic Catalano
F
I'm an a - corn, small and round, Ly - ing on the
C7 F
cold, cold ground. Eve - ry - bod - y steps on me.
C7 F C7
That is why I'm cracked, you see. I'm a nut, (tsk, tsk) in a
F C7 F
rut! (tsk, tsk) I'm a nut, (tsk, tsk) in a rut!

I'm an a - corn, small and round, Ly - ing on the
cold, cold ground. Eve - ry - bod - y steps on me.
That is why I'm cracked, you see. I'm a nut, (tsk, tsk) in a
rut! (tsk, tsk) I'm a nut, (tsk, tsk) in a rut!
tsk tsk
Turn page for another verse.

Try singing these words to the tune "I'm a Nut." Keep the same beat when you add all the rattles and beeps; just make the line longer.

I'm a little piece of tin.
Nobody knows the shape I'm in.
Got four wheels and a running board.
I'm a four-door, I'm a Ford.
Honk honk! (Rattle, rattle, rattle, crash, beep, beep!)
Honk honk! (Rattle, rattle, rattle, crash, beep, beep!)
Honk honk! (Rattle, rattle, rattle, crash, beep, beep!)
Honk honk! Honk honk! Honk honk!

Now try to do these silly movements as you sing the words:

Honk honk!

pull your earlobes

rattle, rattle, rattle

shake your head from side to side

crash

tap yourself on the head

beep, beep

gently pinch your nose

Bend and Stretch
Traditional Children's Song
Art by Bonnie MacKain
D G D
Bend and stretch, reach for the stars.
G D A7 D
There goes Ju - pi - ter, here comes Mars.
G D
Bend and stretch, reach for the sky.
G D A7 D
Stand on tip - py - toe, oh! so high.

Bend and stretch, reach for the stars.
There goes Ju - pi - ter, here comes Mars.
Bend and stretch, reach for the sky.
Stand on tip - py - toe, oh! so high.

It's Time to Get Up!

Army Bugle Call • Art by John C. Wallner

Chorus: It's time to get up, it's
time to get up, it's time to get up in the
morn - ing. It's time to get up, it's
time to get up, it's time to get up to - day.
Turn page
for verse.

Verse: I have a new a - larm clock. It
wakes me with a big shock. In-
stead of go - ing tick - tock, it
clam - ors "clang, clang, clang!"

Verse: I have a new a - larm clock. It
wakes me with a big shock. In-
stead of go - ing tick - tock, it
clam - ors "clang, clang, clang!"
Repeat chorus.

Three Little Piggies

American Folk Song • Art by Brian Lies

Once was a sow who had three lit - tle pig-gies.___

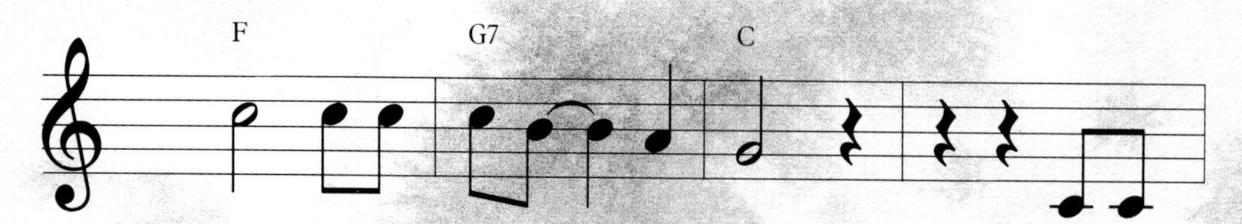

Three lit - tle pig-gies__ had she. And the

old sow al - ways went, “Oink! Oink! Oink!” And the

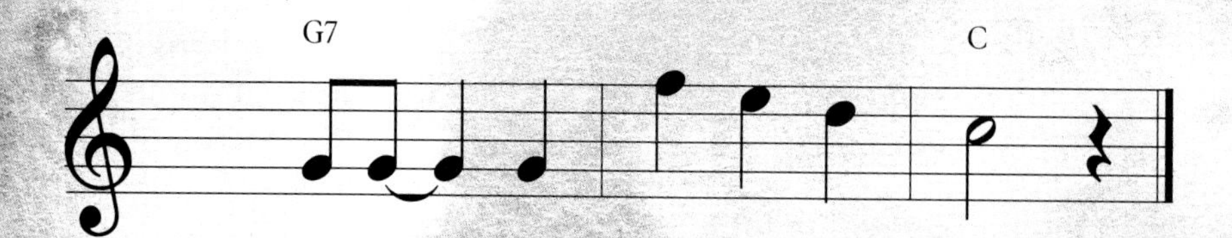

pig-gies__ went, “Wee, wee, wee, wee!”

Once was a sow who had three lit - tle pig - gies.
Three lit - tle pig - gies had she.
And the old sow al - ways went, "Oink! Oink! Oink!"
And the pig - gies went, "Wee, wee, wee, wee!"

This Little Light of Mine

Traditional Children's Song

Art by Kevin Hawkes

This lit-tle light of mine,___ I'm gon-na let it shine.

This lit-tle light of mine,___ I'm gon-na let it shine.

This lit-tle light of mine,___ I'm gon-na let it shine, let it

shine, let it shine, let it shine.

This lit - tle light of mine,______ I'm gon-na let it shine.
This lit - tle light of mine,______ I'm gon-na let it shine.
This lit - tle light of mine,______ I'm gon-na let it shine, let it
shine, let it shine, let it shine.

Wind the Bobbin Up
D
Wind ___ the bob-bin up, wind ___ the bob-bin up.
G D A7 D
Pull, pull, clap, clap, pull. Point to the ceil-ing,
G D G D
point to the floor, point to the win - dow,
A7 D
point to the door. Clap your hands to-ge - ther now,
G D G D A7 D
One two three. Pat them, pat them on your knee.

Traditional Children's Song • Art by C. L. A. MacKenzie
Wind the bob - bin up, wind the bob - bin up.
Pull, pull, clap, clap, pull. Point to the ceil - ing,
point to the floor, point to the win - dow,
point to the door. Clap your hands to - ge - ther now,
One two three. Pat them, pat them on your knee.
MOUSEPLEX
RULES OF RACE DAY
NO CATS
FINISH

My Hat, It Has Three Corners
Traditional Melody "Carnival of Venice"
C
G7
My hat, it has three cor - ners. ___ Three
C
cor - ners has my hat. ___ And had it not three
G7
C
cor - ners, ___ it would not be my hat. ___

Art by John C. Wallner
My hat, it has three cor - ners. Three
cor - ners has my hat.___ And had it not three
cor - ners,___ it would not be my hat.___

Five brown ted-dies sit - ting on a wall,

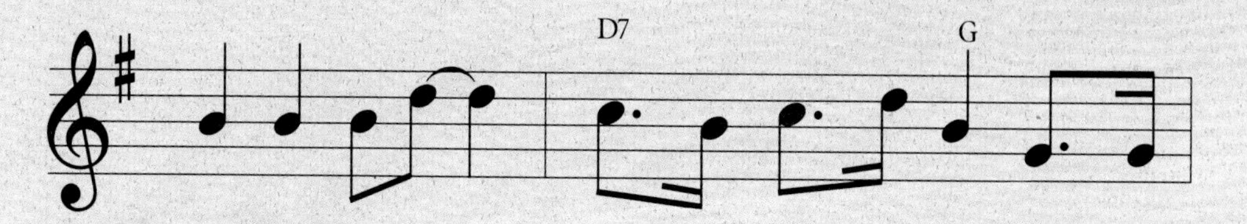

Five brown ted-dies sit - ting on a wall, And if

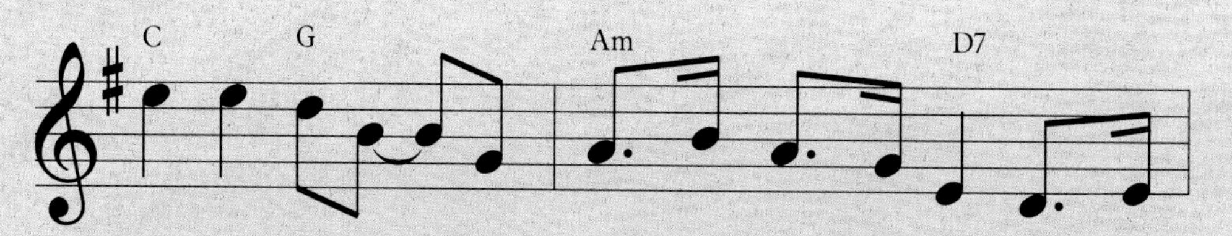

one brown ted - dy should acc - i - dent - 'ly fall, There'd be

four brown ted-dies sit - ting on a wall.

Traditional Children's Song
Art by Rebecca Kelly

Turn the page for more verses.

Four brown teddies, sitting on a wall,
Four brown teddies, sitting on a wall,
And if one brown teddy should accident'ly fall,
There'd be three brown teddies sitting on a wall.

Three brown teddies . . . *etc.*

Two brown teddies . . . *etc.*

One brown teddy, sitting on a wall,
One brown teddy, sitting on a wall,
And if one brown teddy should accident'ly fall,
There'd be no brown teddies sitting there at all!

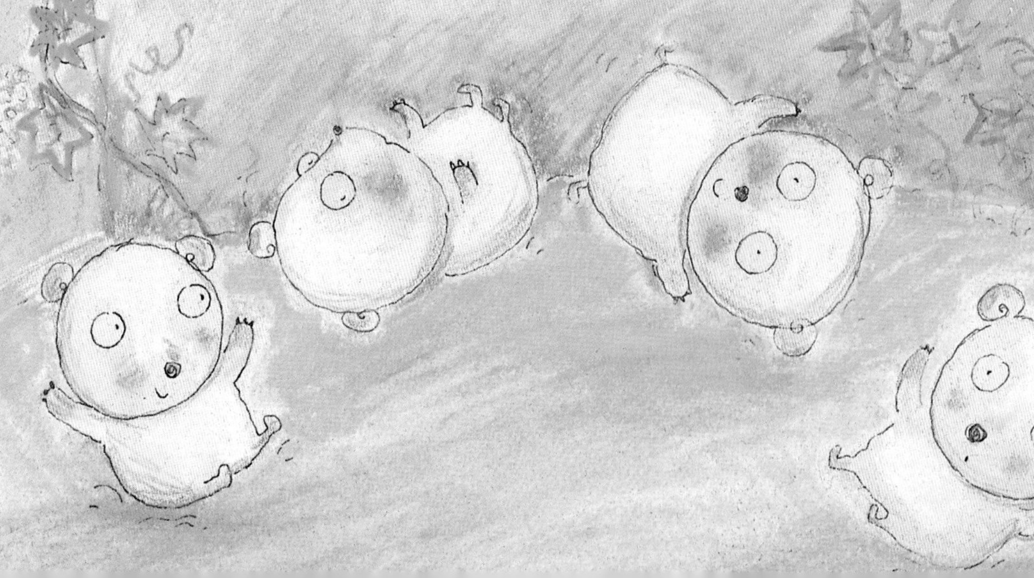

Published by Carus Publishing Company
a division of Carus Corporation
 Printed in Mexico

ISBN 0-8126-0072-X

Grateful acknowledgment is made to the following copyright owners for permission to reprint their material.
Dominic Catalano for "I'm a Nut!" artwork © 1995 by Dominic Catalano.
Kevin Hawkes for "This Little Light of Mine," artwork © 1995 by Kevin Hawkes.
Elizabeth E. Howard for "The Caterpillar," artwork © 1995 by Elizabeth E. Howard.
True Kelley for "Hop, Hop, Hop!" artwork © 1995 by True Kelley.
Rebecca Kelly for "Five Brown Teddies," artwork © 1995 by Rebecca Kelly.
Brian Lies for "Three Little Piggies," artwork © 1995 by Brian Lies.
Bonnie MacKain for "Bend and Stetch," artwork © 1995 by Bonnie MacKain.
Catharine MacKenzie for "Wind the Bobbin Up," artwork © 1995 by Catharine MacKenzie.
Jennifer Plecas for "Buddies and Pals," artwork © 1995 by Jennifer Plecas.
John C. Wallner for "It's Time to Get Up!" and "My Hat, It Has Three Corners," artwork © 1995 by John C. Wallner.
Warner/Chappell Music, Inc. for "Polar Bear and Crocodile," words by David Stevens from *Twice 55 Community Songs,* © 1930 by Summy-Birchard, Inc. All rights reserved.
Nadine Bernard Westcott, Inc. for "Polar Bear and Crocodile," artwork © 1995 by Nadine Bernard Westcott.